Simply Frittata

When Only a Great Frittata Matters

Graziella Montenero

AuthorHouse™ UK Ltd.
1663 Liberty Drive
Bloomington, IN 47403 USA
www.authorhouse.co.uk
Phone: 0800.197.4150

Published by AuthorHouse 09/11/2013

ISBN: 978-1-4918-7693-0 (sc)
978-1-4918-7692-3 (e)

authorHOUSE®

Table of Contents

Introduction

Although I write in English, I am Italian. I live in a city near Rome. I was born and grew up in San Valentino, a little town close Napoli, in South Italy. All I can cook comes from that area and from my family, mainly from my mum, Emma, who cooks delicious dishes every day.

While preparing an Italian cookbook that will be published soon, I decided to make a separate small cookbook for the Italian frittata. This dish is fun to prepare, quick, and easy. At the same time, it is tasty and healthy; that is why every Italian loves it so much.

We consider the frittata to be the symbol of the humble and poor cuisine because it is an inexpensive dish, and you can make it with whatever you have in the fridge or the pantry. Eggs are always the main ingredient, and you can add any kind of vegetable, meat, or cheese.

My family and I used to make a frittata when we were in a hurry or when we needed to recycle leftover vegetables from lunch or dinner the day before. We combine them with eggs and other ingredients, cook the egg mixture with a specific method for a few minutes—and that's all. We also make amazing, delicious *frittatas* with leftover pasta.

A frittata can also be a complete meal in itself; the ingredients, simple and wisely combined, give us all that our bodies need. Indeed, most Italians like to eat a frittata for lunch or dinner as the perfect light meal. However, our frittatas are also great for picnics because they can be eaten warm or at room temperature.

Before you start to cook the Italian frittata, I'd like to give some suggestions.

First of all, in order to prepare a delicious frittata, I recommend using the best, freshest eggs you can find. I prefer to buy eggs at local farms that use natural methods to raise the hens.

I suggest using fresh, natural vegetables; it is important to use some ingredients only when they are fresh or you risk a change in the flavor of your frittata. For example, I suggest using parsley and mint only when fresh; if you can't find them fresh, do not use them at all. Every time I have been abroad and used dried parsley or dried mint, my dishes were not the same. The food tasted differently.

Most of our frittatas are traditionally cooked in a skillet on the stove, but a few are oven-cooked. However, except for the oven-cooked frittata, I always suggest pouring the egg mixture into a nonstick - skillet that is generously oiled and already hot.

When it's time to flip the frittata, use a lid larger than the skillet.

You can make a frittata as thick as you like; I love thick frittata, and I usually use a smaller skillet so it comes out thicker.

Frittata is a very versatile dish; once you master the recipe, you will have fun making it. You may get creative and try some other versions by using whatever ingredients you have on hand.

Artichokes Frittata

Frittata di Carciofi

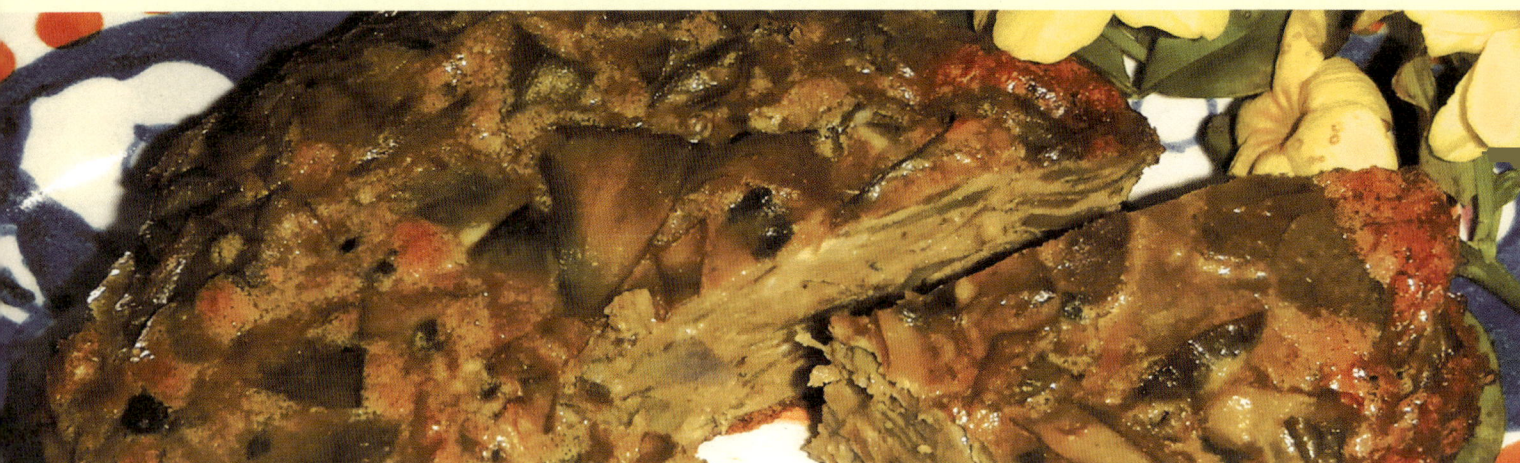

While many enjoy the flavor of artichokes, few have had the opportunity to experience the diversity found in Italian cooking. If the artichokes are fresh, tender, and cooked the right way, they will taste great. You will be pleasantly surprised by the delicious, luxurious flavor. This frittata is one of the most popular recipes with artichokes.

Preparation time: about 20 minutes
Cooking time: about 15–20 minutes
Serves: 2–3

Ingredients:

4–5 fresh artichokes
1 tbsp. extra virgin olive oil
1 garlic clove, peeled and finely chopped
½ cup (120 ml) warm water
1 tbsp. freshly minced parsley

Salt (about ¾ tsp. total)
6 eggs
6 tbsp. grated Parmigiano Reggiano (or Grana
    Padano) cheese
3 oz. (80 ml) cottage cheese

Method:

1. Wash the artichokes thoroughly with cold tap water. Remove the leaves from the outside of each artichoke until you arrive at the pale inner leaves. Using a large knife, cut off the top of the artichokes and throw it away. Then peel the base and remove any residual hard parts of the leaves. Cut each artichoke in half lengthwise, remove the purple leaves and the hairs (if there are any) that cover the heart, and finely slice them.
2. In a large pan, sauté the garlic in extra virgin olive oil and add the artichokes, warm water, parsley, and a pinch of salt. Cover and cook about 15 minutes or until the artichokes are tender. Turn off the heat (make sure the water has evaporated) and set aside.
3. Meanwhile, in a bowl, lightly beat the eggs, add Parmigiano cheese, ½ tsp. of salt, cottage cheese, and artichokes. Mix well.
4. Heat a large, nonstick, oiled skillet,[1] and pour in the egg mixture. Shake the pan gently or use a spatula to distribute it evenly over the surface. Cover and cook the frittata on low heat for a few minutes until the bottom is light golden-brown[2] and the top has started to firm up. Then flip onto a large lid and slide it back into the pan to cook the other side.
5. Slide onto a serving plate and serve with toasted or hard bread.[3]

---

[1] Some people find it easier to use a smaller skillet to make 2–3 frittatas instead of 1 large one.
[2] You can check by lifting the edge of the frittata with a fork.
[3] You may need to season with salt.

Asparagus and Bacon Frittata

Frittata di Asparagi e Pancetta

This frittata is a perfect meal because it's healthy, nutritious, and tasty. It has a bit of everything— protein, carbohydrates, and vegetables.

Preparation time: about 30 minutes
Cooking time: about 15–20 minutes
Serves: 3–4

Ingredients:

1 tbsp. extra virgin olive oil
½ onion, peeled and finely chopped
½ lb. (220 g) asparagus, chopped
1 cup (250 ml) water
Salt (about ¾ tsp. total)
¼ lb. (110 g) bacon, diced
6 eggs
7 tbsp. grated Parmigiano Reggiano (or Grana Padano) cheese
Vegetable oil (just enough to generously oil the skillet)

Method:

1. Sauté the onions in the extra virgin olive oil. Add the asparagus, water, and a pinch of salt. Cover and cook until the asparagus is tender. Then, add bacon and cook together for another 5–6 minutes (make sure the water has evaporated). Set aside.
2. In a bowl, lightly beat the eggs with cheese and ½ tsp. of salt. Add the onions, bacon, and asparagus mixture. Mix well.
3. Heat a large, nonstick, oiled skillet[1] and pour in the egg mixture. Shake the pan gently or use a spatula to distribute it evenly over the surface. Cover and cook the frittata on low heat for a few minutes until the bottom is light golden-brown[2] and the top has started to firm up. Then flip onto a large lid and slide back into the pan to cook the other side.
4. Slide onto a serving plate and serve warm or at room temperature with toasted bread.[3]

---

[1] Some people find it easier to use a smaller skillet to make 2–3 frittatas instead of 1 large one.
[2] You can check by lifting the edge of the frittata with a fork.
[3] You may need to season with salt.

Basic Frittata
Frittata di Base

What is amazing about Italian cooking is the simplicity of it. This dish is one of the best examples: it's simple, quick, and delicious. It is basically just eggs, milk, and cheese.

Preparation time: 5 minutes
Cooking time: about 15–20 minutes
Serves: 1–2

Ingredients:

3 eggs
4 tbsp. grated Parmigiano Reggiano (or Grana Padano) cheese
2 tbsp. milk
Salt (according to taste)
Vegetable oil (just enough to generously oil the skillet)

Method:

1. In a bowl, lightly beat the eggs with cheese, milk, and a pinch of salt. Mix well.
2. Heat a large, nonstick, oiled skillet[1] and pour in the egg mixture. Shake the pan gently or use a spatula to distribute it evenly over the surface. Cover and cook the frittata on low heat for a few minutes until the bottom is light golden-brown[2] and the top has started to firm up. Then flip onto a large lid and slide back into the pan to cook the other side.
3. Slide onto a serving plate and serve immediately with a green salad and toasted bread.[3]

---

[1] Some people find it easier to use a smaller skillet to make 2–3 frittatas instead of 1 large one.
[2] You can check by lifting the edge of the frittata with a fork.
[3] You may need to season with salt.

Broccoli Frittata

Frittata di Broccoli

Eggs, cheese, and broccoli create a flavorful combination. Like most Italian frittatas, this is easy to prepare and very cheap. You might make it with things you already have in the house or with the vegetables leftover from lunch or dinner the day before.

Preparation time: 10–15 minutes
Cooking time: about 15–20 minutes
Serves: 2–3

Ingredients:

About 4 cups (1 L) water
Salt (about 1 ½ tsp. total)
½ lb. (approx. 250 g) broccoli, cut into large pieces
5 eggs
5 tbsp. grated Parmigiano Reggiano (or Grana Padano) cheese
Pepper to taste
¼ cup (60 ml) heavy cream
1 tbsp. all-purpose flour
Vegetable oil (just enough to generously oil the skillet)

Method:

1. Bring a pot of water with 1 tsp. of salt to a boil. Add broccoli to the boiling water and cook for 10–12 minutes or until tender. Drain with a colander. Then cut them into smaller pieces and mash a little bit with a fork.
2. Meanwhile, in a large bowl, beat the eggs with cheese, ½ tsp. of salt, and pepper. Add heavy cream and broccoli and mix well. Add flour and stir again.
3. Heat a large, nonstick, oiled skillet[1] and pour in the egg mixture. Shake the pan gently or use a spatula to distribute it evenly over the surface. Cover and cook the frittata on low heat for a few minutes until the bottom is light golden-brown[2] and the top has started to firm up. Then flip onto a large lid and slide back into the pan to cook the other side.
4. Slide onto a serving plate and serve with bread.[3]

---

[1] Some people find it easier to use a smaller skillet to make 2–3 frittatas instead of 1 large one.
[2] You can check by lifting the edge of the frittata with a fork.
[3] You may need to season with salt.

Cauliflower Frittata

Frittata di Cavolfiore

This is a nutritious and healthy vegetarian frittata; it is so flavorful that even meat eaters will love it. Your guests will not leave your house without the recipe in hand.

Preparation time: 10–15 minutes
Cooking time: about 20–25 minutes
Serves: 3–4

Ingredients:

About 4 cups (1 L) water
Salt (about 2 tsp. total)
1 lb. (450 g) cauliflower, cut into large pieces
7 eggs
4 tbsp. grated Parmigiano Reggiano (or Grana Padano) cheese
About 2 oz. (60 g) cheddar cheese, finely chopped
½ cup (120 ml) heavy cream
2 tbsp. all-purpose flour
Nutmeg to taste
Pepper to taste

Method:

1. Bring a pot of water with 1 tsp. of salt to a boil. Add cauliflower to the boiling water. Cook for 10–12 minutes or until tender. Drain with a colander. Then cut into smaller pieces.
2. Preheat oven to 390° F (200° C). Line a baking dish with baking paper.
3. Meanwhile, in a large bowl, beat the eggs with Parmigiano cheese, add cheddar cheese, heavy cream, flour, 1 tsp. of salt, nutmeg, and pepper. Then add the cauliflower and stir well.
4. Pour the egg mixture into the baking dish and use a spatula to distribute it evenly over the surface. Bake for 20 minutes or until frittata is set[1] and the top is light golden-brown.
5. After the frittata has rested for a few minutes, serve with a side dish of fresh green salad (dressed with extra virgin olive oil, salt, and fresh lemon juice) and a glass of good red wine (if desired).[2]

---

[1] You can check by lifting the edge of the frittata with a fork.
[2] You may need to season with salt.

Chard Frittata
Frittata di Bietola

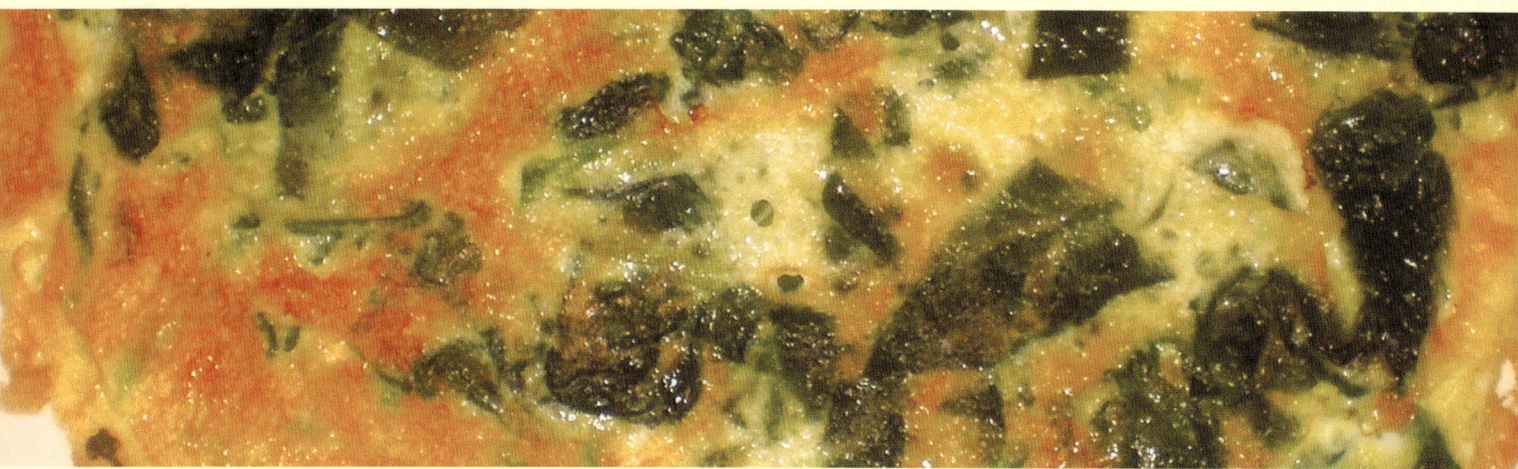

This frittata is one of my favorite. Combining a large amount of chard with cheese and eggs makes the dish delicious and very healthy. Like most of the Italian frittatas, it's a perfect meal for those who are vegetarians.

Preparation time: 10 minutes
Cooking time: about 15–20 minutes
Serves: 2–3

Ingredients:

About 8 cups (2 L) water
Salt (about 2 ½ tsp. total)
1 lb. (450 g) fresh chard
5 eggs
4 tbsp. grated Parmigiano Reggiano (or Grana Padano) cheese
1 tbsp. all-purpose flour
Vegetable oil (just enough to generously oil the skillet)

Method:

1. Bring a large pot of water with 2 tsp. of salt to a boil. Add chard to the boiling water and cook for 7–8 minutes or until tender. Drain with a colander; then chop and mash a little with a fork.
2. Meanwhile, in a bowl, lightly beat the eggs with cheese and ½ tsp. of salt. Add chard and mix well; then add flour and stir.
3. Heat a large, nonstick, oiled skillet[1] and pour in the egg mixture. Shake the pan gently or use a spatula to distribute it evenly over the surface. Cover and cook the frittata on low heat for a few minutes until the bottom is light golden-brown[2] and the top has started to firm up. Then flip onto a large lid and slide back into the pan to cook the other side.
4. Slide onto a serving plate and serve warm or at room temperature with toasted bread.[3]

---

[1] Some people find it easier to use a smaller skillet to make 2–3 frittatas instead of 1 large one.
[2] You can check by lifting the edge of the frittata with a fork.
[3] You may need to season with salt.

Country Frittata
Frittata Rustica

A few ingredients and some fresh ripe tomatoes are all you need to make this quick summer frittata. It will taste great if you use the tastiest, freshest tomatoes you can find.

Preparation time: about 20 minutes
Cooking time: about 20–25 minutes
Serves: 3–4

Ingredients:

2 tbsp. extra virgin olive oil
1 medium white onion, peeled and chopped
3 oz. (80 g) bacon, diced
½ lb. (220 g) fresh ripe tomatoes, finely chopped
Salt (about ¾ tsp. total)
7 eggs
Pepper to taste
A bunch of basil leaves
About 2 oz. (60 g) cheddar cheese, chopped

Method:

1. Sauté the onion in the extra virgin olive oil, add bacon, and cook until crispy. Then add tomatoes and cook for another 8–9 minutes. Season with a pinch of salt and set aside.
2. Preheat the oven to 390° F (200° C). Line a baking dish with baking paper.
3. Meanwhile, in a bowl, lightly beat the eggs with ½ tsp. of salt and pepper. Add the mixture of onion, bacon, and tomatoes to the eggs and mix well. Add basil and cheddar cheese and stir again.
4. Pour the egg mixture into the baking dish and use a spatula to distribute it evenly over the surface. Bake for 20 minutes or until frittata is set[1] and the top is light golden-brown.
5. After the frittata has rested for a few minutes, serve as a main course with a glass of chilled white wine (if desired).[2]

---

[1] You can check by lifting the edge of the frittata with a fork.
[2] You may need to season with salt.

Fall Frittata

Frittata d'Autunno

This frittata is the perfect fall meal: it is a mix of different mushrooms, ham, eggs, and cheese. It's a good alternative to the most popular frittata; everyone I've prepared it for loves it.

Preparation time: 20–30 minutes
Cooking time: about 15–20 minutes
Serves: 2–3

Ingredients:

2–3 tbsp. extra virgin olive oil

¼ lb. (110 g) ham, diced

2 garlic cloves, peeled and finely chopped

A mix of fresh flavorful mushrooms (about 1 lb. or 450 g), sliced

1 tbsp. freshly minced parsley

Salt (about 1 tsp. total)

6 eggs

5 tbsp. grated Parmigiano Reggiano (or Grana Padano) cheese

1 tbsp. black peppercorns

Vegetable oil (just enough to generously oil the skillet)

Method:

1. In a large pan, heat the extra virgin olive oil. Add the ham and brown on all sides. Transfer to a bowl and set aside.
2. In the same pan, sauté the garlic until it begins to brown. Add mushrooms and parsley, season with ½ tsp. of salt, and cook until the mushrooms are tender and the cooking liquid has evaporated.
3. In a bowl, lightly beat the eggs with cheese, ½ tsp. of salt, and peppercorns. Add ham and mushrooms and mix well.
4. Heat a large, nonstick, oiled skillet[1] and pour in the egg mixture. Shake the pan gently or use a spatula to distribute it evenly over the surface. Cover and cook the frittata on low heat for a few minutes until the bottom is light golden-brown[2] and the top has started to firm up. Then flip onto a large lid and slide back into the pan to cook the other side.
5. Slide onto a serving plate and serve warm or at room temperature with toasted bread.[3]

---

[1] Some people find it easier to use a smaller skillet to make 2–3 frittatas instead of 1 large one.
[2] You can check by lifting the edge of the frittata with a fork.
[3] You may need to season with salt.

Frittata of Pasta

Frittata di Pasta

This frittata, also named Pastiera, is an amazing pasta recipe because, as you will see, it is a big exception to all the rules of cooking pasta properly. The dish originated in Napoli, and it was mainly prepared when there was leftover pasta from lunch or dinner. It originated as a way to recycle leftover food.

Today, it is tradition to eat Frittata of Pasta on the Saturday before Easter and on Pasquetta, Easter Monday, but we also make it quite often during the year. My family and I make the following recipe; it can be made ahead of time and is the perfect meal to take to picnics.

Salami is an optional ingredient, but if you decide to use it, I highly recommend using authentic Italian salami. Select the best quality you can find because bad-tasting salami can affect the whole Frittata of Pasta.

Preparation time: about 30–40 minutes
Cooking time: about 40–50 minutes
Serves: 4–5

Ingredients:

About 10 cups (2 ½ l) water
Salt (about 1 ½ tbsp.)
1 lb. (450 g) pasta (a mix of spaghetti and bucatini)
4 eggs
1 cup (250 ml) freshly grated Pecorino Romano cheese
2 oz. (60 g) Italian salami, diced
1/3 cup (80 ml) extra virgin olive oil
Pepper to taste
Vegetable oil (just enough to generously oil the pan)

Method:

1. Bring a large pot of water to a boil. Then add salt and pasta. Cook, stirring often, about three times longer than the cooking time indicated on the package.[1]
2. When pasta is done, drain with a colander, pour into a very large bowl, and let rest until it's cold.[2]
3. Add eggs, cheese, salami, oil, and pepper. Stir and mix well all the ingredients with the pasta.[3]
4. At this point, heat a large, nonstick, oiled pan.[4]
5. Pour pasta into the pan, making a thick layer (2–2 ½ inches or 5–6 cm) and gently press over it with a fork. Then cover and cook over medium heat until the bottom is golden brown (about 20 minutes).
6. Then flip over onto a large lid and slide back into the pan to cook the other side.
7. Serve warm or cold.

---

[1] The pasta will absorb almost all the water.
[2] You can cook it the day before. When cold, pasta will stick together. Don't worry; with the addition of the other ingredients, you will be able to untie it.
[3] It will take a little work to mix the ingredients and to untie the pasta.
[4] Some people find it easier to use a smaller pan to make 2–3 Pastieres instead of 1 large one.

Frittata with Eggplant, Ham, and Blue Cheese

Frittata con Melanzane, Prosciutto e Gorgonzola

This frittata is rich and tasty. The simple combination
of eggs with eggplant, ham, and a touch of blue
cheese creates a luxurious flavor.

Preparation time: about 15 minutes
Cooking time: about 15–20 minutes
Serves: 2–3

Ingredients:

2 medium eggplants, chopped
Salt (about 2 ¼ tbsp. total)
3 tbsp. extra virgin olive oil
¼ lb. (110 g) ham, diced
2 oz. (50 g) blue cheese
6 eggs
2 tbsp. grated Parmigiano Reggiano (or Grana Padano) cheese
Vegetable oil (just enough to generously oil the skillet).

Method:

1. Generously salt (about 2 tbsp.) the eggplant and let them sit in a bowl for about an hour. Then rinse and squeeze them by hand to remove the bitter water.
2. At this point, in a small pan, heat the extra virgin olive oil, add the eggplant, and cook for about 20 minutes or until they soften and brown a little. Season with salt, transfer to a bowl, and set aside.
3. Put the ham in the pan and brown it. Add the blue cheese to the ham, mix well, and cook for another few minutes or until the cheese melts.
4. Meanwhile, in a bowl, lightly beat the eggs with Parmigiano cheese and ½ tsp. of salt. Then add the eggplant and the mixture of ham and blue cheese and mix well.
5. Heat a large, nonstick, oiled skillet[1] and pour in the egg mixture. Shake the pan gently or use a spatula to distribute it evenly over the surface. Cover and cook the frittata on low heat for a few minutes until the bottom is light golden-brown[2] and the top has started to firm up. Then flip onto a large lid and slide back into the pan to cook the other side.
6. Slide onto a serving plate and serve as a main course with a light white wine (if desired).[3]

---

[1] Some people find it easier to use a smaller skillet to make 2–3 frittatas instead of 1 large one.
[2] You can check by lifting the edge of the frittata with a fork.
[3] You may need to season with salt.

Frittata with Ham, Cheese, and Arugula

Frittata di Prosciutto, Formaggio e Rugola

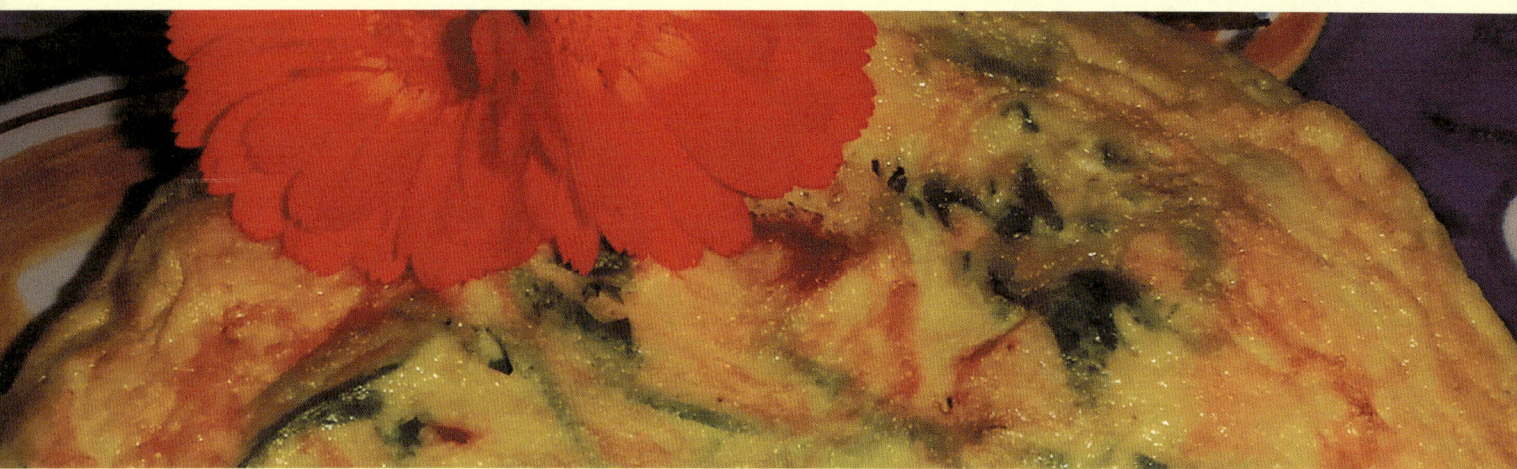

This is one of the easiest frittatas and has a remarkable flavor. It's perfect for a fast, nutritious meal.

Preparation time: 10 minutes
Cooking time: about 15–20 minutes
Serves: 2–3

Ingredients:

1 tbsp. of butter
¼ lb. (110 g) ham, diced
5 eggs
Salt (about ½ tsp.)
Pepper to taste
¼ lb. (110 g) smoked cheese, finely diced
A bunch of spicy arugula leaves
Vegetable oil (just enough to generously oil the skillet)

Method:

1. In a small pan, melt the butter over low heat. Add the ham and brown it a little. Set aside.
2. Meanwhile, in a bowl, lightly beat the eggs with salt and pepper. Add ham, smoked cheese, and arugula. Mix all the ingredients.
3. Heat a large, nonstick, oiled skillet[1] and pour in the egg mixture. Shake the pan gently or use a spatula to distribute it evenly over the surface. Cover and cook the frittata on low heat for a few minutes until the bottom is light golden-brown[2] and the top has started to firm up. Then flip onto a large lid and slide back into the pan to cook the other side.
4. Slide onto a serving plate and serve immediately.[3]

---

[1] Some people find it easier to use a smaller skillet to make 2–3 frittatas instead of 1 large one.
[2] You can check by lifting the edge of the frittata with a fork.
[3] You may need to season with salt.

Frittata with Mint

Frittata alla Menta

This recipe shows that simplicity is a virtue. This frittata is simple, light, and quick; it's one of my favorites.

Preparation time: 5 minutes
Cooking time: about 15–20 minutes
Serves: 1–2

Ingredients:

3 eggs
2 tbsp. grated Pecorino Romano cheese
Salt (according to taste)
A bunch of fresh mint leaves
2 tbsp. breadcrumbs
Vegetable oil (just enough to generously oil the skillet)

Method:

1. In a bowl, beat the eggs with Pecorino Romano cheese and a pinch of salt. Then add the mint leaves and the breadcrumbs. Mix well.
2. Heat a large, nonstick, oiled skillet[1] and pour in the egg mixture. Shake the pan gently or use a spatula to distribute it evenly over the surface. Cover and cook the frittata on low heat for a few minutes until the bottom is light golden-brown[2] and the top has started to firm up. Then flip onto a large lid and slide back into the pan to cook the other side.
3. Slide onto a serving plate and serve with toasted bread.[3]

---

[1] Some people find it easier to use a smaller skillet to make 2–3 frittatas instead of 1 large one.
[2] You can check by lifting the edge of the frittata with a fork.
[3] You may need to season with salt.

Frittata with Zucchini Flowers and Ricotta Cheese
Frittata di Fiori di Zucchine e Ricotta

This recipe is one of the most delicious variations to the traditional Frittata with Zucchini. It's light, tasty, and nutritious. I clean the zucchini flowers by removing the stems and nothing else. I don't like to remove the pistils because I find them delicious and tasty.

Preparation time: 5 minutes
Cooking time: about 20–25 minutes
Serves: 2–3

Ingredients:

20 zucchini flowers
3 tbsp. extra virgin olive oil
½ medium onion, peeled and finely chopped
Salt (about ¾ tsp. total)
7 eggs
7 tbsp. grated Parmigiano Reggiano (or Grana Padano) cheese
Pepper to taste
¼ lb. (110 g) ricotta cheese

Method:

1. Clean zucchini flowers by removing the stems. Gently wash them with fresh water.
2. Sauté the onion in the extra virgin olive oil, add the zucchini flowers, and cook for a few minutes. Season with a pinch of salt and set aside.
3. At this point, preheat oven to 390° F (200° C). Line a baking dish with baking paper.
4. Meanwhile, in a bowl, beat the eggs with Parmigiano cheese, ½ tsp. of salt, and pepper. Then add the zucchini flowers and ricotta cheese and mix well.
5. Pour the egg mixture into the baking dish and use a spatula to distribute it evenly over the surface. Bake for 20 minutes or until frittata is set[1] and the top is light golden-brown.
6. After the frittata has rested for a few minutes, serve with a side dish of fresh green salad (dressed with extra virgin olive oil, salt, and fresh lemon juice) and a glass of white wine (if desired).[2]

---

[1] You can check by lifting the edge of the frittata with a fork.
[2] You may need to season with salt.

Garlic Frittata

Frittata all'Aglio

This vegetarian frittata is simple and tasty; it can be a healthy addition to any dish, or it can be served as a light main course.

Preparation time: 5 minutes
Cooking time: about 15–20 minutes
Serves: 1–2

Ingredients:

2 tbsp. extra virgin olive oil
1 head of garlic, separated, peeled, and finely sliced
3 eggs
5 tbsp. grated Parmigiano Reggiano (or Grana Padano) cheese
Salt (according to taste)
Pepper to taste
Vegetable oil (just enough to generously oil the skillet)

Method:

1. In a small pan, heat the extra virgin olive oil and fry the garlic.
2. Meanwhile, in a bowl, lightly beat the eggs with cheese and a pinch of salt and pepper.
3. Add garlic and mix well.
4. Heat a large, nonstick, oiled skillet[1] and pour in the egg mixture. Shake the pan gently or use a spatula to distribute it evenly over the surface. Cover and cook the frittata on low heat for a few minutes until the bottom is light golden-brown[2] and the top has started to firm up. Then flip onto a large lid and slide back into the pan to cook the other side.
5. Slide onto a serving plate and serve immediately with toasted bread.[3]

---

[1] Some people find it easier to use a smaller skillet to make 2–3 frittatas instead of 1 large one.
[2] You can check by lifting the edge of the frittata with a fork.
[3] You may need to season with salt.

Nettles Frittata

Frittata di Ortiche

The combination of healthy vegetables, cheese, and eggs makes a great recipe and a flavorful dish. Take care when handling the nettles because they sting; it will take very little cooking to eliminate the stinging.

Preparation time: 10 minutes
Cooking time: about 15–20 minutes
Serves: 2–3

Ingredients:

About 7 cups (1 ¾ liters) water
Salt (about 2 tsp. total)
1 lb. (450 g) fresh tender nettles
½ onion, peeled and finely chopped
1 tbsp. extra virgin olive oil
6 eggs
4 tbsp. grated Parmigiano Reggiano (or Grana Padano) cheese
Vegetable oil (just enough to generously oil the skillet)

Method:

1. Bring a large pot of water (about 6 cups or 1 ½ liters) with 1 ½ tsp. of salt to a boil. Add nettles to the boiling water and cook for 6–7 minutes. Drain with a colander and then chop them.
2. Meanwhile, cook the onion with the extra virgin olive oil and 1 cup (250ml) of water until soft.
3. Add nettles, stir and cook for 3–4 minutes (make sure the water has evaporated). Set aside.
4. In a bowl, lightly beat the eggs with cheese and ½ tsp. of salt.
5. Add nettles and onions and mix well.
6. Heat a large, nonstick, oiled skillet[1] and pour in the egg mixture. Shake the pan gently or use a spatula to distribute it evenly over the surface. Cover and cook the frittata on low heat for a few minutes until the bottom is light golden-brown[2] and the top has started to firm up. Then flip onto a large lid and slide back into the pan to cook the other side.
7. Slide onto a serving plate and serve immediately with bread.[3]

---

[1] Some people find it easier to use a smaller skillet to make 2–3 frittatas instead of 1 large one.
[2] You can check by lifting the edge of the frittata with a fork.
[3] You may need to season with salt.

Onion Frittata

Frittata di Cipolle

An onion frittata is an inexpensive vegetarian meal, with a strong flavor and very easy to prepare. You can make it for a fancy meal or an everyday meal.

Preparation time: 20–30 minutes
Cooking time: about 15–20 minutes
Serves: 2–3

Ingredients:

3–4 medium white onions (about 1 lb. or 450 g), peeled and chopped
2 tbsp. extra virgin olive oil
½ cup (120 ml) water
Salt (about ¾ tsp. total)
5 eggs
3 tbsp. grated Parmigiano Reggiano (or Grana Padano) cheese
Pepper to taste
4 tbsp. ricotta cheese
Vegetable oil (just enough to generously oil the skillet)

Method:

1. Cook the onions with the extra virgin olive oil and water, until they are soft and begin to brown (make sure the water has evaporated). Season with a pinch of salt and set aside.
2. In a bowl, lightly beat the eggs with Parmigiano cheese, ½ tsp. of salt and pepper; then add onions and ricotta cheese and stir well.
3. Heat a large, nonstick, oiled skillet[1] and pour in the egg mixture. Shake the pan gently or use a spatula to distribute it evenly over the surface. Cover and cook the frittata on low heat for a few minutes until the bottom is light golden-brown[2] and the top has started to firm up. Flip onto a large lid and slide back into the pan to cook the other side.
4. Slide onto a serving plate and serve with grilled vegetables and toasted bread.[3]

---

[1] Some people find it easier to use a smaller skillet to make 2–3 frittatas instead of 1 large one.
[2] You can check by lifting the edge of the frittata with a fork.
[3] You may need to season with salt.

Peas Frittata

Frittata di Piselli

This easy, flavorful frittata is perfect for a light summer meal.

Preparation time: 10–15 minutes
Cooking time: about 15–20 minutes
Serves: 1–2

Ingredients:

2 tbsp. extra virgin olive oil
½ medium white onion, peeled and finely chopped
About 1 cup (250 ml) frozen or fresh peas
Salt (according to taste)
3 eggs
2 tbsp. grated Pecorino Romano cheese
Vegetable oil (just enough to generously oil the skillet)

Method:

1. Sauté the onion in the extra virgin olive oil. Add peas, season with salt, cover, and cook for 5–6 minutes or until tender (make sure you don't overcook them).
2. Meanwhile, in a bowl, beat the eggs with cheese and a pinch of salt. Add the peas and mix well.
3. Heat a large, nonstick, oiled skillet[1] and pour in the egg mixture. Shake the pan gently or use a spatula to distribute it evenly over the surface. Cover and cook the frittata on low heat for a few minutes until the bottom is light golden-brown[2] and the top has started to firm up. Then flip onto a large lid and slide back into the pan to cook the other side.
4. Slide onto a serving plate and serve immediately.[3]

---

[1] Some people find it easier to use a smaller skillet to make 2–3 frittatas instead of 1 large one.
[2] You can check by lifting the edge of the frittata with a fork.
[3] You may need to season with salt.

Porcini Mushrooms Frittata
Frittata ai Funghi Porcini

My family and I love this recipe. This frittata is tasty and elegant; it takes a little more work—and more ingredients—but the flavor is spectacular.

Preparation time: about 1 ½ hour
Cooking time: about 15–20 minutes
Serves: 3–4

Ingredients:

2 oz. (50 g) dried Porcini mushrooms
4 tbsp. extra virgin olive oil
1 onion, peeled and chopped
½ cup (120 ml) white wine
1 ½ cup (370ml) warm water
Salt (about 1 tsp. total)
3 tbsp. pine nuts

½ cup (120 ml) heavy cream
7 eggs
5 tbsp. grated Parmigiano Reggiano (or Grana Padano) cheese
Pepper to taste
Vegetable oil (just enough to generously oil the skillet)

Method:

1. Place the mushrooms in a large bowl, cover with tap water, and let soak for about 4–5 hours. Then drain the water and rinse the mushrooms.
2. In a large pan, sauté the onion gently in the extra virgin olive oil. Add mushrooms and white wine and cook for 10–15 minutes or until the wine has evaporated. Add warm water and ½ tsp. of salt, cover and let simmer for about 1 hour or until the mushrooms are tender (make sure the liquid has evaporated).
3. At this point, add pine nuts to the pan with mushrooms and cook all together for 5–6 minutes. Add heavy cream and cook for another 2–3 minutes. Allow to cool and set aside.
4. Meanwhile, in a bowl, lightly beat the eggs with cheese, ½ tsp. of salt, and pepper. Then add the mushroom mixture to the eggs and mix well.
5. Heat a large, nonstick, oiled skillet[1] and pour in the egg mixture. Shake the pan gently or use a spatula to distribute it evenly over the surface. Cover and cook the frittata on low heat for a few minutes until the bottom is light golden-brown[2] and the top has started to firm up. Then flip onto a large lid and slide back into the pan to cook the other side.
6. Slide onto a serving plate and serve as a main course with red wine.[3]

---

[1] Some people find it easier to use a smaller skillet to make 2–3 frittatas instead of 1 large one.
[2] You can check by lifting the edge of the frittata with a fork.
[3] You may need to season with salt.

Potato Frittata

Frittata di Patate

This is a simple and delicious vegetarian dish. I have made this frittata several times, and my guests have always enjoyed it. My kids also love it.

Preparation time: 10–15 minutes
Cooking time: about 20–25 minutes
Serves: 3–4

Ingredients:

4 tbsp. extra virgin olive oil
2 medium white potatoes, finely diced
Salt (according to taste)
6 eggs
4 tbsp. grated Pecorino Romano cheese
Pepper to taste
4 oz. (110 g) cottage cheese
2 tbsp. freshly minced parsley

Method:

1. Heat the extra virgin olive oil in a skillet. Add the potatoes and fry until crispy and golden. Season with salt and set aside.
2. Preheat oven to 390° F (200° C). Line a baking dish with baking paper.
3. Meanwhile, in a bowl, beat the eggs with Pecorino Romano cheese, a pinch of salt, and the pepper. Add potatoes, cottage cheese, and parsley to the eggs and mix well.
4. Pour the egg mixture into the baking dish and use a spatula to distribute it evenly over the surface. Bake for 20 minutes or until frittata is set[1] and the top is light golden-brown.
5. After the frittata has rested for a few minutes, serve with a green salad or grilled vegetables.[2]

[1] You can check by lifting the edge of the frittata with a fork.
[2] You may need to season with salt.

Spinach and Blue Cheese Frittata
Frittata di Spinaci e Gorgonzola

There are only a few recipes as quick and rich as this one is. The combination of spinach, blue cheese, and eggs makes a frittata that tastes great and is very healthy.

Preparation time: about 15 minutes
Cooking time: about 15–20 minutes
Serves: 2–3

Ingredients:

3 tbsp. extra virgin olive oil
½ medium onion, peeled and finely chopped
½ lb. (220 g) fresh spinach
Salt (about ¾ tsp. total)
2 oz. (50 g) blue cheese
5 eggs
4 tbsp. grated Parmigiano Reggiano (or Grana Padano) cheese
Vegetable oil (just enough to generously oil the skillet)

Method:

1. Sauté the onion in the extra virgin olive oil. Add spinach and a pinch of salt, cover, and cook for 10–12 minutes or until tender.
2. Add the blue cheese to the pan with spinach, stir well, and cook all together for another few minutes or until the cheese melts.
3. Meanwhile, in a bowl, lightly beat the eggs with Parmigiano cheese and ½ tsp. of salt. Then add the mixture of spinach and blue cheese to the eggs and mix well.
4. Heat a large, nonstick, oiled skillet[1] and pour in the egg mixture. Shake the pan gently or use a spatula to distribute it evenly over the surface. Cover and cook the frittata on low heat for a few minutes until the bottom is light golden-brown[2] and the top has started to firm up. Then flip onto a large lid and slide back into the pan to cook the other side.
5. Slide onto a serving plate and serve immediately with bread.[3]

---

[1] Some people find it easier to use a smaller skillet to make 2–3 frittatas instead of 1 large one.
[2] You can check by lifting the edge of the frittata with a fork.
[3] You may need to season with salt.

Spinach Frittata

Frittata di Spinaci

Easy and delicious, this is one of my best frittatas. It is very healthy and nutritious. It's perfect for an unusual lunch or dinner.

Preparation time: 10 minutes
Cooking time: about 15–20 minutes
Serves: 2–3

Ingredients:

About 8 cups (2 L) water
Salt (about 2 tsp. total)
1 lb. (450 g) fresh spinach
6 eggs
8 tbsp. grated Parmigiano Reggiano (or Grana Padano) cheese
Pepper to taste
1 tbsp. all-purpose flour
Vegetable oil (just enough to generously oil the skillet)

Method:

1. Bring a large pot of water with 1 ½ tsp. of salt to a boil. Add spinach to the boiling water and cook for 6–7 minutes. Drain with a colander, then chop and mash a little with a fork.
2. Meanwhile, in a bowl, lightly beat the eggs with cheese, ½ tsp. of salt, and the pepper. Add spinach and mix well, add flour, and stir.
3. Heat a large, nonstick, oiled skillet[1] and pour in the egg mixture. Shake the pan gently or use a spatula to distribute it evenly over the surface. Cover and cook the frittata on low heat for a few minutes until the bottom is light golden-brown[2] and the top has started to firm up. Then flip onto a large lid and slide back into the pan to cook the other side.
4. Slide onto a serving plate and serve warm or at room temperature with bread.[3]

---

[1] Some people find it easier to use a smaller skillet to make 2–3 frittatas instead of 1 large one.
[2] You can check by lifting the edge of the frittata with a fork.
[3] You may need to season with salt.

Spring Frittata
Frittata di Primavera

A Spring Frittata is a good way to get a lot of vitamins and to eat a light meal. This dish is a combination of different vegetables—zucchini, peas, and spring onion—with eggs and cheese.

Preparation time: 10–15 minutes
Cooking time: about 20–25 minutes
Serves: 3–4

Ingredients:

5–6 tbsp. extra virgin olive oil

4–5 small tender zucchini (about 1 lb. or 450 g), sliced very thinly

Salt (about 1 tsp. total)

About 2 cups (500 ml) water

1 spring onion, peeled and finely chopped

1 cup (250 ml) fresh or frozen peas

7 eggs

6 tbsp. grated Parmigiano Reggiano (or Grana Padano) cheese

Method:

1. In a nonstick pan, heat the extra virgin olive oil and fry zucchini. Season with a pinch of salt and set aside.
2. Meanwhile, bring a small pot of water with a pinch of salt to a boil. Add onion and peas and let boil for 3–4 minutes, then lift out with a strainer and set aside.
3. Preheat oven to 390° F (200° C). Line a baking dish with baking paper.
4. In a bowl, lightly beat the eggs with cheese, ½ tsp. of salt, and the pepper. Add zucchini, peas, and onion to the eggs and mix well.
5. Pour the egg mixture into the baking dish and use a spatula to distribute it evenly over the surface. Bake for about 20 minutes or until frittata is set[1] and the top is light golden-brown.
6. After the frittata has rested for a few minutes, serve with bread.[2]

---

[1] You can check by lifting the edge of the frittata with a fork.
[2] You may need to season with salt.

Zucchini Frittata

Frittata di Zucchine

This is a delicious dish that we serve in summer as a light main dish. However, it works any time that zucchini is available. The simple combination of zucchini, eggs, and cheese makes a quick and tasty meal. It is a perfect choice for those who are vegetarians.

Preparation time: 20–30 minutes
Cooking time: about 15–20 minutes

Serves: 2–3

Ingredients:

2–3 small zucchini (about ½ lb. or 220 g), diced
2–3 tbsp. extra virgin olive oil
Salt (about ¾ tsp. total)
6 eggs
8 tbsp. grated Parmigiano Reggiano (or Grana Padano) cheese
Pepper to taste
A bunch of fresh mint leaves (optional)
Vegetable oil (just enough to generously oil the skillet)

Method:

1. Sauté zucchini in the extra virgin olive oil until they are tender and begin to brown. Season with a pinch of salt and set aside.
2. In a bowl, lightly beat the eggs with cheese, ½ tsp. of salt, and the pepper. Add the zucchini and mint and mix well.
3. Heat a large, nonstick, oiled skillet[1] and pour in the egg mixture. Shake the pan gently or use a spatula to distribute it evenly over the surface. Cover and cook the frittata on low heat for a few minutes until the bottom is light golden-brown[2] and the top has started to firm up. Then flip onto a large lid and slide back into the pan to cook the other side.
4. Slide onto a serving plate and serve with bread.[3]

---

[1] Some people find it easier to use a smaller skillet to make 2–3 frittatas instead of 1 large one.
[2] You can check by lifting the edge of the frittata with a fork.
[3] You may need to season with salt.

Index

O
Onion Frittata (*Frittata di Cipolle*) 34

P
Peas Frittata (*Frittata di Piselli*) 36
Porcini Mushrooms Frittata (*Frittata ai Funghi Porcini*) 38
Potato Frittata (*Frittata di Patate*) 40

S
Spinach and Blue Cheese Frittata (*Frittata di Spinaci e Gorgonzola*) 42
Spinach Frittata (*Frittata di Spinaci*) 44
Spring Frittata (*Frittata di Primavera*) 46

Z
Zucchini Frittata (*Frittata di Zucchine*) 48

Graziella Montenero is a lawyer who was born and grew up in a little town close to Napoli, in Southern Italy. She now lives in a city near Rome with her husband and two babies. She enjoys cooking for family and friends, and she spends all her free time cooking and testing new delicious recipes.

Her frittata recipes are current and authentic because she writes directly from the heart of Italy. She has the voice of authentic Italy.

41035635R00033